Rory —

Dream Big

or

Don't Bother!

♡, Jim Lynn

PRAISES FOR
Jerilynn Stephens

"Jerilynn is one of my favorite people. When she sets her mind to something, she makes it happen! I've loved watching her evolve and grow with INTENTION!"

- Robert Herjavec, Star of Shark Tank

"I've worked with Jerilynn for more than 10 years. She is a great example of someone who sets goals, takes action, and achieves it. More importantly she understand that achieving her own goals are not enough. She defines success as taking others with her and helping them reach their goals. If you get the chance to work with Jerilynn, do it !"

- Mark Cuban, Star of Shark Tank

"Jerilynn is a rare gem. She not only has years of experience and talent behind her but, she is one of the most authentic and genuine people I have ever met.

Her willingness to care for and build up those around her isn't something you come across nowadays. She is the type of person who knows lighting another's flame won't dim her own. So, happy to have met her and blessed to call her a friend."

-Chloe Brown, Short Hair Influencer

Instagram @chloenbrown

YouTube- Chloe Brown

THE FIVE

"F" WORDS

TO

MANIFESTING

YOUR LIFE

JERILYNN STEPHENS

This book is dedicated to my amazing husband Danny
and our beautiful son Eli.
Thank you for your love and support always!
Eli, continue to shine the bright light that is you.

CONTENTS

Introduction: *1*

Chapter 1: *F* **Is For Figure it Out**   **13**
            Dream Big or Don't Bother

Chapter 2: *F* **Is For Focus**   **23**
            Where Focus Goes, Energy Flows

Chapter 3: *F* **Is For Fearless Action**   **35**
            Co-Creating with the Universe

Chapter 4: *F* **Is For Feel It**   **49**
            Tap Into Your Power to Manifest

Chapter 5: *F* **Is For Faith**   **59**
            Knowing and Believing

Afterword   *71*

Life Hacks   *73*

Acknowledgments   *79*

About the Author   *83*

INTRODUCTION

What do you really want? Those five words might keep you awake at night. They're why this book exists.

This book was born because of the countless conversations I've had with people from all walks of life who ask me the same question: How do you manifest exactly what you want in life?

The answer is simple: I know how to "F" it.

And no, not *that* F word.

First a quick disclaimer: I laugh when I'm in the middle of these conversations because the truth is I don't manifest *everything* I need or desire. I only wish it was that easy. What I have found out is that it takes a tremendous amount of F's – focus, fearless action and faith (just to get started) to create the life you truly want and not the one that exists between the alarm blaring in the morning and the covers pulled over your head at night.

Manifesting. Let's get right to that word. You've probably heard of it. People toss around the word as in, "I believe in the power of manifesting because I created the person of my dreams or that amazing job." Sounds great, right, but exactly how did they do it? The truth is many have no idea what manifesting really means. Manifesting is quite powerful and basically means that we are responsible for creating our world and our reality. Does it work? Yes – and then some. Most of the time what I manifest in my own life is ten times bigger, stronger, more powerful and glorious than I ever imagined. Nice? Absolutely. Daunting? That's a big yes.

This book, for instance, was born because I was entering my sixteenth season of working on a top television series as the head hairstylist. I was at that point when a milestone birthday was approaching and I began reflecting on how blessed I am and how far I've come. It caused me to think, "What more can I do? What more can I give?" Writing a book wasn't even close to being on any list. All I wanted to do was help people by sharing my experiences of how I came to be the Hollywood Hairstylist. Little did I know this desire would blossom into a platform of teaching, speaking and writing.

My transformation occurred by working what I call **The Five F Words**. These are actually five beautiful words that always bring me back to my truth. They were born during a conversation I had with a friend who wanted to know my method to manifesting my desires. She didn't just want a few helpful hints, but a step-by-step guide that she promised to follow in order to dramatically change her own life.

How did I do it? What I did was manifest sobriety, productivity, a loving marriage and the job of my dreams to name a few major life goals. The truth was I had been manifesting what I wanted for a long time when it came to both my career and personal life. As I thought about what specifically I do when I want to manifest something, off my tongue rolled . . .

<u>**The Five F Words to Manifesting Your Life:**</u>

FIGURE

FOCUS

FEARLESS ACTION

FEEL IT

FAITH

You can't go wrong when you combine the fierce F's. I'm a living, human example of how it works time and time again.

My practice is a culmination of years of study in what I like to call The Art of Manifestation. It started when I was getting sober at the age of thirty-three. I've always been quite open about my struggles with sobriety over the years and a journey to wellness that has included some heartache, stress and struggles. That's life. It's messy, scary, beautiful, joyful, boring, dull, exciting and unpredictable. It is everything and more than one could ever expect. One quick warning: Manifesting with The Five F Words will not take away all hardships you may encounter. What it will do is put you in the driver's seat with a clear map of where you are going and how you will get there. Think of the Five F words as your GPS.

INTRODUCTION

As I was getting sober, I was determined to slay my demons and start living a productive and happy life. To that end, I devoured every self-help book I could get my hands on. My favorites are on my website – www.jerilynnstephens.com. These books opened a whole new world for me, one where I was no longer a victim of circumstance, but a powerful co-creator of my life. I'm proud to say I have been sober for quite a few years and will continue on this sober journey, one day at a time. In the past, I did tell myself my life was so good that I could try it again. *"Don't worry. It was just a bad time in your life. You have a great marriage and family now. You can handle it."* If you've ever struggled with addiction you know what I'm talking about here. Life is going great and we tell ourselves, "Just one won't matter." That may be true, but the issue is it's never just one. And that's the problem.

What does this have to do with manifesting?

Sobriety has given me the clear head and heart to take healthy risks and go after my dreams. This book isn't about how to get sober as there are plenty of resources for that journey. What I can tell you is what took me years to manifest when I was drinking, took weeks or months when I was sober. Why? To manifest, you need a head that's clear and a soul that's happy. You cannot manifest consciously if you are disconnected from life.

Ask yourself: Do I have a crutch in my life that is keeping me from achieving my dreams? It doesn't have to be a substance abuse issue. It can be a toxic relationship, a victim mentality or simply you're much too busy and/or too tired to take control of your life.

As my sobriety progressed, I learned more about the power of manifestation. I wasn't just intrigued by it, but became obsessed. A small part of me was skeptical, but I still thought, "If this is true, I want to know how to do it and then have some fun with it." I didn't want to just read about manifesting, but wanted to test the principles in my own life. I didn't begin with a major life shifter either. All I wanted was some new ski equipment although I didn't have the money to buy it. When I found myself in beautiful Mammoth, California where I really wanted some gear in order to ski. I decided to just go for it, just do it and all those other great slogans.

Yes, I bought the equipment before I had the money to pay for it. I know, I know. It was a scary move and not one I suggest people try. There was risk involved because if my little experiment failed, I was the one who would suffer with a high interest credit card rate I'd be facing as I paid off my new equipment. That didn't stop me from making my purchase knowing deep in my heart that somehow – someway – the money would be replenished. I did have a WTH moment because even when you live in faith, doubt creeps in. Yet, I knew enough about manifesting, even in those early days, to redirect my thinking back to knowing the Universe has my back.

So, I took a leap of faith and the Universe did not disappoint. When I got home, there was an email asking if I was available to work on a commercial for *the exact amount* I just spent. That was the first of many WOW manifestation moments I have experienced in my life.

What I have learned since then is manifestation and co-creation (more on that in later chapters) isn't always about manifesting material objects. You can also manifest peace, harmony, right relationships, health and well-being or basically anything you want. My greatest realization is that WE are all powerful co-creators of our own lives. All of us have access to this universal power to manifest the life of our dreams. Whether you are familiar with the world of manifestation or not, I encourage you to take this practice and implement it in your life to empower yourself and others. The principles I'll provide in this book have been around for over a hundred years and possibly longer. I did not create them; they are the culmination of my years of study, practice and experimentation. Like all of us, I have learned from those who have gone before me. It is my hope in sharing my knowledge that I may help anyone interested in tapping into their unlimited potential for co-creating the life of their dreams.

For ease of learning and practice, I have laid out The Five F Words in a specific order; however, when you are consciously manifesting, you will find that each process happens in no particular order. They are circular and work together simultaneously except for the first "F" Word – **FIGURE** -- which is always first because if you don't know where you're going, how will you know when you get there?

These Five F Words encourage you to make bold moves and go in the direction of your dreams. As with anything new, I suggest you begin by utilizing the steps in order, but once the practice is in place, you will notice how each action supports the whole.

Begin by reading the book from cover to cover, doing the exercises and establishing the practices needed for conscious co-creation with the Universe. Start small as you build your manifestation muscle. I suggest you keep a manifestation journal to chart your progress. Please do not get discouraged if change is not as quick as you would like. All acquired skills take practice, patience and more practice. When you're waiting for big shifts, remind yourself again and again: You deserve to live the life of your dreams!

Dream Big or Don't Bother

This bold statement became a defining affirmation for me when I began consciously manifesting. At the time, my career was expanding and evolving into what I had been dreaming of since beauty school. Another amazing turn was when my husband miraculously manifested into my life in 2007. As I became more and more aware of how everything was lining up, the phrase "Dream Big" kept getting louder and louder in my head. One day, out loud and proud, I said to no one in particular: "Dream Big or Don't Bother." Since 2011, this has been part of my email signature and it is how I live my life every single day.

It wasn't always this way. I was that little girl void of big dreams. I didn't really struggle – or at least I thought. I didn't even know I was lost until much later in life. Before that revelation, I was simply existing with what life gave me, drifting along and accepting crumbs when I wanted the whole cake.

Most of us drift in this life, allowing the limitations

of past experiences and the opinions of others to keep us down. After countless years of self-help books and support groups, I finally realized I was my biggest obstacle. My self-worth -- or the lack of it -- was ultimately keeping me from fully embracing my "crazy" dreams, which weren't really that crazy at all. Life can only give you what you allow it to give you. So, when I say, "Dream Big or Don't Bother," what I mean is to GO FOR IT!

For years, I didn't think I was worthy. I wasted a lot of time feeling disempowered or convinced that somehow my dreams didn't matter, or they were too big or not big enough. I even had moments where I thought, "Who do you think YOU are to have these dreams? How dare you think that YOU deserve that kind of money, success or recognition." These thoughts weren't taking center stage in my mind, but were unconsciously just there. How did I know I thought so poorly of myself? The answer was in my actions, relationships and what I was willing to accept.

If you are feeling any of these things, don't waste another second settling for a life that is not supporting your dreams. Life is short and you were born at this time and in this place to shine. Dream Big or Don't Bother!" I live this affirmation every day and I invite you to do the same. Light up! The world needs you!

I love this quote from Marianne Williamson, "*Our deepest fear is not that we are inadequate. Our deepest fear is that we are powerful beyond measure. It is our Light, not our Darkness, that most frightens us.*"

Turn the page to turn on the light.

CHAPTER

1

F IS FOR FIGURE

FIGURE Out What You Want

Dream Big or Don't Bother

Figuring out what you want is the most important step in manifesting the life of your dreams. It is from this platform that all of the magic happens. When figuring out what you want, it is extremely important to be as clear as possible. Webster's dictionary has a few definitions of clarity and I think this one stands out above the rest: *The quality of being coherent and intelligible.* If you are not clear about what you want, how are you going to co-create with the Universe? We are always manifesting; the difference now is you can do it consciously as the co-creator of your life. Don't get me wrong because there are circumstances beyond our control that happen to all of us. The difference is when you are manifesting the life of your dreams then circumstances, pleasant or not, don't matter because you are now empowered to make choices that move you in the direction of your dreams.

It was early on in my manifestation journey where I learned the value of clarity. I knew I wanted to get married, so I began figuring out exactly who this dream guy would be. I wanted a tall, dark, handsome man and more importantly, one who loves his family. Since I was dreaming big, I said he has to be rich, too. One night when I was out with friends, I told them I did indeed manifest a good guy, but he wasn't ambitious or rich. We all burst out laughing like schoolgirls. The Universe did indeed give me what I had asked for – a man named Rich.

The Universe has a sense of humor!

This experience taught me the keys to manifesting consciously. Though Rich was a good guy, he wasn't my guy. So, I went deeper than my surface desire and discovered even though I wanted someone who was rich, what I really wanted was financial freedom. I had narrowed it down, but it was still not clear enough for the Universe as financial freedom means a lot of things to a lot of people. What did it mean for me? I had to dive deep and do the work to get clear and specific on what a financially free life meant for me. It wasn't just about not being broke. For me, it meant no budgets or having to ask the question, "Can I afford this?" It means I attract the funds to easily and effortless pay for all of the necessities, luxuries and incidentals required to live life on this planet.

When I dove below the surface of my desires, I realized I wasn't looking for a man to take care of me. I was looking for my life partner who would be ambitious, thrive in his work and love his family. I am happy to report, we have found each other. We've been married for twelve years and have a beautiful son. He's everything and more than I could ever have imagined. I live in gratitude every day for the life we have built together.

Whether it's financial freedom, a rich man or peace on earth you desire, be clear and specific and take the time to dive below the surface to explore the depths of your desires.

If you are having a hard time being specific, ask yourself, *"What am I afraid of?"* I have found most people are afraid of limiting or blocking their options and think by claiming very specifically what they want that somehow, they might miss out on something bigger. If you aren't honest with yourself and the Universe by claiming unapologetically what you want to exactly manifest then you will be left with what you get and not with what you truly desire.

Figuring Out What You Don't Want Can Help You Figure Out What You Do Want

In the course of most lives, we go through a period when we are not sure what to do next. There is a transition happening and we feel stuck and insecure. If you find yourself in this spot, not to worry. Take a piece of paper or grab your computer and list all the things you don't want. Write down at least ten things and it doesn't matter what they are because the purpose of this exercise is to open you up and get your creative juices flowing. Go for it and don't hold back as this is for your eyes only.

Once your list is complete, look at it and ask yourself, *"Okay, if this is what I don't want then what is it I do want?"* If you are still not sure, the below exercise will help you gain clarity on what you do want. The answers may not come in this moment, but keep asking the question. I promise one day it'll come to you and you will know what it is you truly want. The "a-ha" moment will appear in a split second. For me, it was when I walked on my first film set and just *knew* this is where I wanted to be. What

I didn't know at the time is the Universe was aligning to help me reach my goals.

You Deserve It

Believing you are worthy is especially important when manifesting the life of your dreams. Many of us don't really believe we deserve the success we desire. It's not a conscious belief, but it reveals itself in our choices and behaviors. For instance, we settle for what shows up because we think we can't have what we really want. Don't ever settle for crumbs when you can have the whole cake. The best antidote for feelings of unworthiness is a huge dose of self-love. Try being your own best friend. Whenever negative self-talk rears its ugly head, push it aside and reply with a positive answer fit for your BFF.

Questions to Get Your Juices Flowing

These questions are designed to help you find clarity when it comes to what it is you truly want to manifest. Keep your answers in your manifestation journal and reread it often. Modify, as needed, and don't ever give up. Ask yourself:

1. What does your life look and feel like if you were fearless and knew you couldn't fail?

We all know stories of people who have overcome insurmountable odds and they did it because they knew -- without a doubt -- what they wanted to achieve. Don't let the committee in your mind keep you from dreaming big. Everything you see in this world was once just a mere thought, so go for it. You have nothing to lose and everything to gain. New mindset: There is plenty on this earth, so why not you?

2. What type of lifestyle do you want?

Do you want to move or stay where you are currently living?

What kind of house do you live in or is it an apartment?

What kind of neighborhood do you live in?

Do you have help with the kids?

Do you want kids?

Are you married?

Do you want to travel?

3. What does your career look like?

Do you want to be the boss, own your business or work for someone else?

Do you have several income streams or just one?

Are you a stay-at-home mom or dad?

Figuring out what you want doesn't end when you manifest your desires. It's a lifelong journey and one that will change as the years go by. When I reflect on my own life and see the wonders that have manifested, I'm in awe of how I went from co-creating my dream of being a Hollywood hairstylist to now stepping completely outside my comfort zone and dare I say…a bestselling author and an influential empowerment speaker. WOW – did I just write that? The truth is this is one of the scariest things I have ever done, and sometimes I wonder, *"What am I doing?"* It's normal to freak out about the magnitude of your goals. Think of it this way: You are being called to play a bigger game. If it's not scaring you, then it's not big enough. It's in these "freak out" moments, I sit in faith and know the Universe has my back and is always conspiring for my highest good.

FIGURE ENHANCERS	FIGURE BLOCKERS
Figure out what you don't want	Feeling not worthy
Dive below the surface of what you want to understand the bigger and broader picture of your desire	Lack of clarity and certainty
Stay positive in your thoughts and actions	Staying in negative thinking

NOTES

IS FOR FOCUS

FOCUS On What You Want

Where Focus Goes, Energy Flows

ocus is simply a sustained period of setting your attention on something, which can be challenging in this crazy world of constant stimulation. That is why meditation (more on this in a later chapter) is so important because in addition to connecting you to something greater than yourself, it also builds your focus muscles.

Thoughts Become Things

Every person has their own definition of reality due to the fact that we see life through the lens of our own individual thoughts and beliefs. If you are not sure what beliefs you hold, then look around you as they are being projected back to you in every interaction, every reaction, every thought and every word you say. The good news is that when you change your thoughts, you also change your entire world.

Experts say we have between 12,000 to 60,000 thoughts in a given day. Ninety-five percent of them are recurring, which means we are thinking the same thoughts over and over again. It's these repetitive thoughts that create our beliefs and our reality. However, unfortunately for most us, eighty percent of those thoughts are negative. Yes, I repeat… eighty percent, which means most of us dwell in negativity.

When it comes to the Laws of Attraction, we know that like attracts like. It follows then, that if you're focusing on all of the obstacles in your life and stuck in why you can't do this or have that, then all you will ever see are obstacles. Begin by paying attention to where you spend most of your time focusing. If you are focusing on negative thinking and this is your life-long pattern then you will receive negativity in your life. If you focus on love, you will get more love. If you focus on what you don't have, you get more of that, too. No good comes from living in this pool of "I can't" or "it won't".

I was teaching at a conference and there was a woman in the audience who explained she had been trying to get into the hair union in Los Angeles. She was focusing on working with union people who unfortunately could not help her until she was actually in the union, which was a Catch-22. To qualify for the Local 706 union, you need to work paid, non-union jobs at least sixty days per year for three years in a five-year period. It is a bit daunting and a great accomplishment once achieved, but she wasn't there yet. In fact, she was discouraged and felt something was blocking her. Every time I tried to give her the solution, which was to work with non-union people, she kept saying, "But, but, but…" She couldn't hear what I was saying because she already made up her mind that it was far too difficult, if not impossible, for her to get into the union.

We all do that in our own lives when it comes to bigger goals. We get so attached to our viewpoint that we are completely blind to the infinite possibilities present all around us. If something is not working for you or you feel blocked, ask the question, *"What am I not seeing here?"* Allow your heart and mind to explore options you never knew existed. When the woman in the audience finally had a breakthrough, it was because she had learned to adjust her focus.

Where Focus Goes, Energy Flows

It has been said the strongest force in the Universe is the human will. I don't know if it's true or not, but this statement always intrigued me. What I do know is wherever I put my focus and attention is where my energy goes. I always demonstrate the power of this idea when I'm on a stage speaking. I'll take off my necklace and hold it motionless in front of me while I concentrate on making the necklace move to my will. It does freak some people out, my husband and son included, but this is one of the best examples of how energy flows where focus goes. You can do it, too. It's not a trick. It's actually unseen energy waves generated by your brain that make the necklace move. This is commonly called pendulum magic or dowsing and has been around for hundreds of years. (You can find out how you can use the pendulum in your own life by clicking the book section on my website)I ride a Harley, Yes, I love to ride. It's freeing and fun! I was a passenger on my husband's Harley for years and when our son was big enough, he started going along for rides. Never one to be left on the side of the road, I figured out quickly I needed to have my own Harley. While learning to ride a motorcycle, my instructor told me to keep my eyes pointed in the direction I wanted to go. "Where you focus is where your bike will go," he said.

It was great advice that went beyond riding hogs. In other words, don't stare at the curb because you don't want to hit it. This doesn't just happen with Harley's; it also happens in cars. You may have noticed when you're looking at something on the side of the road, your car drifts in that direction without any effort on your part. This is because we always go in the direction of our focus. If you don't like the direction you're going then change your focus. Everything in this world already exists; it is where we put our focus and attention that ultimately manifests in our lives.

What Are You Focusing On?

We have an amazing opportunity to choose each day what we want to focus on. Starting tomorrow, when you wake up in the morning, notice the thoughts running through your mind. Are you thinking negative thoughts before you even get out of bed? If you're already dreading the day before it even begins then you are setting yourself up for a dreadful day. Take a moment every morning to consciously choose the thoughts that will occupy your mind. If they are not thoughts that support your dreams and desires then you have the power to change them. We are what we think, so think good thoughts.

A fun exercise and a great way to train your brain is to try for at least twenty-four hours to think and say only positive thoughts. The minute a negative thought enters your mind or negative words escape your lips, change it or them to a positive thought or words. This is a fun activity that builds self-awareness and is a learned skill that will enhance the lives of both adults and children. Practice, practice, practice…until you've perfected positivity.

What is Motivating You

It's important to understand what is motivating you in your quest to manifest consciously. Motivation and focus go hand in hand because without motivation, we can easily lose focus. This is why eighty percent of New Year's resolutions fail by February. Most people never fully understand their motivation behind their goals and dreams.

I recently had an "a-ha" moment when I was on a mission to lose weight and look my best for an on-camera job. I did the work, figured out what I wanted, focused and took fearless action. I began to feel myself at my ideal weight and I had faith it would happen. I spent six weeks eating clean and cross training. When it was time to film the show, I had lost eight out of the twelve pounds, which was not the finish line, but I was happy, I felt great and that was enough because it's not about the number, but how you feel. By the way, I felt healthy, fit and beautiful!

Once the filming was over, I noticed I was eating a piece of candy here and a small sliver of cake there, plus my portions became larger. Before I knew it, I was gaining the weight back prompting me to wonder, "What happened?" The truth was I lost my motivation, which was not to lose weight; it was to look and feel amazing on camera. Once my mission was complete, my motivation began to fade. When your focus begins to fade, remind yourself of your WHY.

Remembering your reason for manifesting what you want to manifest is a great way to reactivate your motivation. If your why has been accomplished, but your manifestation process is not complete, create a new why. For me, my weight loss goal was not complete, but my reason for losing weight had passed, I created a new why – which is to look and feel my best at a moment's notice. When the next event or on-camera opportunity shows up, I'll be camera and life ready.

Remember Your Destination

Sometimes, we get caught up in overwhelming details, which in turn can be demotivating. Remember everything is temporary, and it's important to stay focused even if everything in your outside world seems out of alignment with your dreams. Don't give up because success often is right around the corner. Allow setbacks to happen knowing that they're lurking. If you feel discouraged, scared or stuck, it's fine to recognize those emotions, but never, ever let moments of discouragement keep you from creating the life of your dreams. Think of it as opportunity to course correct. Imagine your car is drifting into the other lane. You may have a moment of panic, but with a slight turn of the wheel, you are right back on track.

Focus Enhancers	Focus Blockers
Course correcting when you lose focus	Distractions that don't support your goals and dreams
Develop your willpower Manage your thoughts	Buying into your negative thoughts
Deep understanding of your underlying motivation	Unwilling to see things differently

NOTES

CHAPTER 3

F IS FOR FEARLESS

Take FEARLESS Action

Co-Creating with the Universe

O nce you figure out what you want, you must take fearless action to activate the co-creation process in connection with the Universe. Even if you're not sure what you want or are having trouble focusing on your dreams and goals, you will still take fearless action.

What I have learned about F.E.A.R is it masquerades as *False Evidence Appearing Real.* You know what I mean because we've all been there, worrying and anxious about something that never happens. If it does, it's rarely as big, as dark or as messy as our minds have led us to believe it will be.

Fear is just one more thing in life and like all experiences, we get to define it or let it define us. Don't get me wrong, some fear is good. Its purpose is to protect us from danger, but most of the time the danger we fear is only in our minds.

Slaying Fear

When I find myself in fear, I walk straight into it head on and tell fear I'm here! Buying a Harley and taking riding lessons scared the crap out of me, but I had to do it. Another time I headed straight into fear, I decided to take surfing lessons and be an uber cool mom while enjoying the experience with my son rather than watching him from the beach. I'll never forget the first time heading into the ocean with my wetsuit on, board in hand and following the instructor and my son. I was like . . . *WTH am I doing? Am I crazy?* However, as I felt the cool water on my feet, I began giving myself a pep talk -- quietly of course. "Here you go. You can do this. Just don't think of sharks . . . the shadows are only you," I told myself, adding, "Walk right into that cold water and jump on that board. Paddle, paddle, paddle!"

A friend of mine dives headfirst into her fear. She imagines a pool of water and jumps into the feeling of being afraid. As she comes up through the water, the fear dissipates. Whether you choose to dive into fear or walk straight through it, it doesn't matter. What does matter is you do whatever it takes to move to the other side of fear and never let it become an obstacle that keeps you from living the life of your dreams.

What is Fearless Action?

Fearless action doesn't mean you are **not** afraid; it means you gather all the courage you have and do it anyway. It's not a straight line, but a windy road with peaks and valleys. It's putting yourself out there, doing the work and having the confidence to ask for what you want.

There is a PA (production assistant) I work with on a reality competition show and her story is a perfect example of what it means to take fearless action and co-create with the Universe. Her dream is to be a writer for television, and like so many of us with big lofty goals, she wasn't sure how she was going to get there. She did know if she was on a studio lot, any lot -- Universal, Sony, Warner Brothers, etc. – then she would be in the vicinity of her dreams. When she heard about a company who hires security guards for all of the studios, she applied. I know, crazy. Being a security guard doesn't even come close to being a scripted writer on a television series, but if I learned anything from co-creating my life with the Universe, it's when you show up and let go of the outcome, you are on your way. The next step is to own your dream unapologetically. This is how the unseen energies of co-creation come together in ways your mind could never imagine. But, back to the PA who was soon hired to be a security guard for a big reality competition show.

As a security guard, you're out and about and watch people coming and going. Every day, she would see this guy who was always running, literally dashing from point A to point B. On this particular day, he was walking, and for no apparent reason said, "Hey, no jogging today?" In the course of their short conversation, she learned he was a producer. In that moment, she gathered all her courage and took fearless action by casually saying, "If you ever need a PA, I'd love to apply."

"Sure," he said. "Send me your resume."

It turned out, he was an executive producer or the guy who did the hiring. She was soon hired to be a PA, and with the help of the Universe, co-created the next step on her road to manifesting her dreams. How did she do it? She showed up, worked hard and took fearless action, which sent signals to the Universe that she was serious about her dreams. She was now working in production on a reality competition show. It was not quite the writer's room of her dreams, but an amazing opportunity to learn production in the high stake's world of TV. This knowledge is extremely valuable as a scripted writer.

In this world of instant gratification and shortcuts, I've seen too many people try to make it to the finish line without running the race. It's your participation in the race that allows the Universe to co-create with you in ways you can never imagine.

Look for Synchronicities

Synchronicities are life's seemingly random events that seem related, but are not explained. These include randomly meeting the perfect people to help you on your manifestation journey. We all experience this phenomenon; some just label it as a coincidence. There is one huge difference between coincidence and synchronicity. Coincidence is described as a chance encounter; synchronicity is defined as a deeper intelligence at work. As random as it all may seem, I don't believe it is by chance, but by the grace of divine intelligence that works to co-create with us in realizing our dreams. For me, synchronicities are the language of the Universe. I like to think of it as God and my angels talking to me and letting me know I'm on the right path. In these moments, I realize I'm not alone and there is a whole world, seen and unseen, conspiring for my highest good.

The same is true for you!

Synchronicities come together to show us we are on the right path. For me, it was the unexpected meeting of four woman who would catapult me into my dream career. The first one I met while sitting in a sauna, minding my own business, when a conversation began with the woman sitting next to me. In the course of our chit-chat, she asked me what I did for a living, I told her I was a hair and makeup artist. She told me she was a producer for Getty Images. OMG! My heart just about jumped out of my chest. It never occurred to me I could work there; this is one of the largest stock photography companies in the world and I just met the woman who hires their hair and makeup people. Of all the unexpected places, I ran into her at the spa IN the sauna. This was synchronicity at its best.

She gave me her card and asked if I had a portfolio. Of course, I did. I was prepared for this opportunity although I just had absolutely no idea how, when or where it would manifest. We set up a meeting for the following week. I showed up looking professional with my portfolio in hand, excited and nervous at the same time. Little did I know this opportunity would be the one to catapult me into my film and TV career. Not only did I get the job working for Getty, but I also met two makeup artists and a hairstylist who would change the course of my career forever.

Take a detailed look around you. There are synchronicities lining up and opportunities presenting themselves every day. It's your job to be open to the signs and random meetings. Say yes to everything, except if your intuition sends a strong signal to say no. One rule: Make sure it's not just FEAR talking to you. Take even the smallest of jobs, as you never know who you are going to meet. Do not sit on the sidelines in life. Each time you venture out into the world for any reason, it could be life changing in the most magical way.

Create An Action Plan

What do you need to have in place in order to make your dreams come true? An action plan is not set in stone, but is fluid and changes as needed. The plan's purpose is to give you direction and meaning while keeping you focused. An action plan can be as elaborate or as simple as you want it to be. Think of it as a list of actions you must focus on to be prepared for opportunities and synchronicities when they present themselves.

I also like to create vision boards as a tool. A vision board can be electronic as in Pinterest boards or you can do it old-school style with a poster board where you create a visual representation of your goals and dreams using pictures from a variety of sources, but mainly clipped magazine photos or printed pics from the Internet. Either way, start writing your goals down and begin identifying where you're going to direct your focus. Laser focus on the areas you choose will ultimately accelerate the energy needed to co-create your dream life with the Universe, so choose wisely. Focus on the tasks and skills needed to achieve your dreams.

Once you figure out what you want, you will let go of the outcome. Why? The answer is because the endgame will be bigger and brighter than anything you can ever imagine.

Educate Yourself

I'm not talking degrees here although they are very useful. What I'm talking about is learning skills and acquiring knowledge whenever possible. Knowledge puts you in the driver's seat and education allows you to elevate your talents and craft the highest standards possible. Ask yourself: What steps do I need to take in order to make my dream happen? Add them to your action plan and or vision board. For example, I knew long ago that having extra skills would make me more marketable, which is why I went to makeup school and worked as a makeup artist.

There is a direct link between education and the amount of money you can make over a lifetime. Again, I'm not talking degrees here, I'm pointing at knowledge, information, certifications, etc. What skills do you need to be the best you can be? You must go out and acquire them. All of the above also applies to every area of your life and not just your career. For instance, I have a friend who was going through a divorce with a narcissist. After months of getting nowhere with their settlement, she finally dove in and watched every video, listened to every podcast and read every book on how to negotiate with a narcissist. She gathered her notes, her knowledge and her confidence and set out to the mediator's office. This time was different because she knew who she was dealing with and a month's worth of work manifested in just a few hours. In the end, she got everything she wanted and more. What did she do? She learned who she was dealing with and educated herself on how best to deal with him. She figured out what she wanted, focused on it and then took fearless action to get it.

Sometimes we must learn things we never imagined learning in order to achieve what we want in life. My friend now knows more about narcissists than she ever thought possible, but this invaluable information is forever hers and no one can take it away. No matter where you are in your life and in your career, the key is to never stop learning.

Discernment in Your Sharing

When taking fearless action, there is a delicate line you must balance between shouting your plans from the rooftop and telling no one at all. This is a crucial step that, unfortunately, I learned the hard way. What I know now is don't spill your guts to people who you know will project their own limitations onto you. They are like lobsters. Did you know you don't need to put a lid on a basket holding two lobsters because each time a lobster tries to crawl out of the basket his "buddy" will pull him back down.

Ask yourself: Who are the people in your life pulling you down? If you don't know then I suggest you start paying attention to the lobsters in your life.

You can figure out and focus on what you want, but that's just part of the process. It's fearless action that prepares you for the realization of your dreams. If you are not prepared to realize your goals, you may encounter setbacks that can be hard to overcome. One of my favorite quotes is: *"Luck is what happens when preparation meets opportunity."*

The more prepared you are, the more aware you will become of the synchronicities happening in your life. This is your dream; treat it like the precious thing it is.

Fearless Action Enhancer	Fearless Action Blockers
Knowledge and education	Paralyzing fear
Action plan. Breakdown steps in small steps/tasks	The "lobsters" in your life
Dive or walk straight through your fear	Too busy, no time

NOTES

CHAPTER

F IS FOR FEEL IT

FEEL IT As if It Already Exists

Tapping into Your Power to Manifest

eelings are our internal guide that help us navigate the world we live in. They remind us of what we like and what we don't. They are powerful beyond measure and determine the state of our body, mind and soul.

When you are communicating with the Universe, it's not only your words, but how you feel that inspires co-creation. The more vibrant and clear your feelings are about what you want to manifest, the stronger your connection will be to the Universal Life Force that is always co-creating with us. If you are not connected to your feelings, I suggest you work on connecting now

What now takes days to manifest took years in the days when I drank. I believe it's because my drinking numbed me to my true feelings. It created a veil between me, the world and ultimately the Universe. I didn't know it at the time, but my feelings weren't clear and pure, but instead muddled and distorted.

If you are dependent on a substance or two or three, whether it's alcohol, cannabis, pharmaceuticals, caffeine, sugar or anything else that may alter your mind, body and spirit, I highly suggest taking time away to give yourself the opportunity to experience a clear, true connection to yourself, the world and ultimately the Universe.

If you find yourself struggling, there are groups and communities you can join to help you break the pattern of addiction.

Feel It into Existence

How do you "feel" your dreams and desires into existence? The feeling I'm talking about is when you are on fire, in love and excited beyond belief. It's that high state of knowingness and anticipation. This is similar to the feelings that stir when something you always wanted is about to happen. Every cell in your body is suddenly vibrating so powerfully you feel as if you're going to burst with happiness.

To activate these feelings, think of a light switch you turn on and off. When you turn the light on, infuse every cell of your body with a knowingness and feel as if whatever you want already exists, in the NOW, not sometime in the future, but NOW, as if it is your current reality. I know this can be hard for some and I encourage you to feel as if your dreams already exist. This should happen even in the face of no agreement and if everything in your reality says otherwise. Whatever you want to be, whatever you want to do, feel it NOW. The more intensely you feel it, the more alive it will become.

Create an Affirmation

Create a personal affirmation using I AM. These are two extremely powerful words and when said out loud are communicating to the Universe and to the world what you believe to be true. You are claiming ownership when you say these words as you're opening the portal of possibilities. You're inviting opportunities to show up and lead you along the path of your dreams.

My personal affirmation was I AM a Hollywood Hairstylist. Now, it's I AM an Influential Empowerment

Speaker and Bestselling Author. Will this happen? I don't know, but what I do know is that something bigger and better than what I can ever imagine will happen.

What is your I AM?

Take a moment and write down all your I AM's. These are empowering statements that light up every cell of your body when you say them. Create an I AM for every area of your life: work, family, health, finances, etc. Some examples: I AM a loving and understanding wife; I AM patient and tolerant around my children; I AM a team player; I AM healthy, happy and wise; I AM the CEO of my own company. There is no right or wrong here. It's whatever you want to be in life as long as you just keep it an empowering statement.

Let Go of the Outcome

The beauty in co-creating with the Universe is we don't have to know how it's going to happen, when it's going to or where it's going to happen. We just know that it *will* happen.

I've always been an animal lover and visualized a house full of love, kids, dogs and cats. When I married my husband, I knew he had allergies, but always thought we would "figure it out." When my son became a toddler,

I learned he was also allergic to cats and dogs. I love my husband and son, but I must admit, for a minute, I was truly disappointed. My mind raced with thoughts that ranged from "are you kidding me" to "it's going to be an empty life without animals." My heart grew heavy…for only a moment because deep down I knew somehow, someway, there were animals out there we could all live with.

Over the next few years, we compiled a list of contenders and it wasn't long before I learned I'm not a reptile or small rodent mom, much to the dismay of my son.

Life will always throw us curve balls and circumstances will show up that we didn't plan. It's always our response to the situation that dictates our future. We get to choose who we are going to be and how we're going to respond. I responded by nixing the reptile and rodent plan, but also by acting as if and feeling the love and energy of a pet in the house. I would do this at random times, letting go of the outcome and trusting the perfect pet would manifest for our family.

I was discerning in who I told this to because the odds of having any animals in the house were a long shot. I had no idea if, when or how any of this would show up.

I just knew it would. Then one day my husband found an animal we could all love and live with – PIGS! Yes, we have two micro mini potbelly pigs, Lucy and Ricky, which have grown up to be seventy-five and one hundred and fifty pounds and are seven-years-old.

Pigs, like dogs, come in all shapes, sizes and temperaments. We lucked out with two loving pigs who are the perfect pets for our family. I wouldn't trade them in for the world. My dream came true, but one word of caution. If I was attached to the outcome of having dogs and cats, I would be missing out on the love that is shared with these incredible creatures. Pigs are not for everyone, so please do your research as they require a lot of attention, care and grow bigger than what some breeders will tell you.

What Does Seeing Have to do With Feeling

Visualization is an important part of feeling it because when we pull up an image in our mind, it interprets it as real-life action. Take a moment right now and visualize whatever you want to manifest; it can be big or small. As you see your desire in your mind's eye, I want you to become one with the image, hear the sounds, smell the scents and even feel the temperature. Transport yourself there as if it is happening NOW. Turn the light switch on and FEEL the excitement, the anticipation and the knowingness that this is YOURS. Feel it in your every cell of your body . . . the feeling of accomplishment and the feeling of having your dreams manifest into reality. It's here, it's yours and you did it! As you feel excited about manifesting the life of your dreams, touch your heart and feel that excitement in every fiber of your being. Say out loud your I AM affirmation as you feel it in your heart, body and soul while seeing it with your mind's eye.

Do this exercise every morning upon waking and every evening before you go to sleep. Imagine what it feels like when you achieve the life you always dreamt of living and connect to that feeling pulsating in your body. Once the feeling is magnified throughout your entire being, touch your heart. Remember to do this twice a day for three weeks to anchor the feeling. When you want to enjoy that feeling again, touch your heart to turn the light switch on.

Feel It Enhancer	Feel It Blockers
Visualizing and feeling it in present moment	Drugs and alcohol
Creating your "I AM" affirmation	Not believing it can happen to you
Act as if it actually happened mindset	Controlling the how, when, where it will happen

NOTES

CHAPTER 5

F IS FOR FAITH

FAITH

Knowing and Believing

Faith is your own personal belief about what you know to be true, regardless of what anyone else says. Like your dream, it is a precious thing and it is where light and love reside. Faith is simply a "knowing" in your heart and soul that no matter what is going on in your life, everything will work out for the highest good of all.

When you are in faith, you believe -- regardless of any doubt in yourself or in your dreams. Faith reminds us we are not alone and fuels the energy of co-creation with the universal energy some call God, the Universe or a Higher Power.

Faith is a very personal subject and the last thing I want to do is to turn anyone off with this "F" word. If you already have faith, then you know the magic it creates. If you are new to faith, I ask you to take a moment and consider the possibility of a universal unseen energy assisting you in co-creation that is bigger and brighter than we can ever be.

My own relationship with faith has evolved over the years. I didn't grow up religious and I didn't believe in God. I wasn't quite an Atheist, but I certainly had my doubts about that, too. It was while I was getting sober that I discovered the connection that ignited the faith in me.

My sponsor told me to meditate and pray, but as hard as I tried, I just wasn't connecting. I didn't feel anything differently and certainly didn't feel connected. In fact, I almost gave up when she said to me, *"Do it anyway. Act as if you believe in a power greater than yourself."* I prayed and meditated for months, connecting to the Universe and acting as if I believed, even when I didn't. Then one day: WHAM!

I was sitting there like I had been for months and the most incredible feeling came over me. It was a sensation that's hard to describe, but one where my whole body suddenly filled with love and light. I knew in that exact blissful moment I was not alone and that no one is ever alone. All of sudden, I knew in my heart there is a divine universal intelligence always conspiring for us and for our highest good. When you believe, there are things that start to happen including the synchronicities and the alignment of opportunities. It will actually get to the point where you can't help but to believe. Even if you don't get that sensation at first, try and try again until you find your faith, which is life changing. Start to recognize the power of the energy around you to co-create your dreams.

Crisis of Faith

Sometimes we have a crisis of faith, where we question the validity of everything. If you ever find yourself in this hollow, dark place then just allow yourself to feel everything you feel. Don't judge yourself or others too harshly because I promise you will find your balance again.

My dear friend went through a crisis of faith during a tough couple of years. Eventually, she began to wonder if the concept of God was made up to help us mere mortals cope with the struggle, we call life. She was angry, so she blamed God. After twenty-four hours of questioning everything she had ever been told, taught and believed, she woke up and knew faith had not abandoned her. She had abandoned faith. She told me faith would not let her go. Even when she doubted the reason for existence, the universal energies conspired for her highest good. What happened to make her believe again? A simple act of kindness without any judgment, restored her faith. Look for the signs around you that point you directly toward your faith. It's your job to recognize and grasp them while holding them dearly to your heart.

Faith as Fuel

Faith is fuel for manifesting and though it is the fifth "F" word it, I truly feel it is the foundation for this entire practice. Once you figure out what you want, you must have the faith it will happen. I like to think of faith as an energy or a high vibe feeling that is directly connected to the divine energy of allowing instead of doing. Think of it this way: Figuring out what you want requires doing something; faith is a core belief that requires nothing but believing.

Igniting Faith

Having faith in yourself is especially important when manifesting the life of your dreams. Believe and know deep in your heart and soul you deserve the success you desire. Be aware of self-sabotaging behaviors, thoughts and toxic people. Remember those are the lobsters in your life.

I highly encourage you to start a daily practice to strengthen your faith and connect to your soul, your heart and the Universe. Your practice can be meditation, prayer or hikes in nature -- anything that allows you to get out of your head and into your heart. I know it can be challenging to find the time to shower, let alone meditate or take hikes. Remember connecting to the Universe through your heart and soul is essential to co-creating the life of your dreams.

When you are meditating, praying or find yourself present in nature, communicate with the part of yourself that knows no doubt, no fear and no anxiety. This is the you that knows you are worthy of having your dreams and desires manifest. No matter what happened in the past or is going on right now, YOU ARE WORTHY! Say it to yourself until YOU BELIEVE it. I AM WORTHY. This mindset transforms disempowering beliefs into empowering ones.

Begin by quieting your mind, but don't try too hard. The very act of trying is what makes it difficult. There is no right or wrong way to meditate, but here is a simple practice I do. Breathe in fully with big belly breaths. Breathe in through your nose and out through your mouth. When you count the breaths in and count the breaths out, your brain has no choice except to be in that moment. You won't have a chance to think about dinner, work or what's bothering you. If those types of thoughts creep in, just go back to your breath and counting. Once you establish a rhythm, usually after a few minutes, you can then imagine a laser beam starting from deep inside of your belly. Bring the laser beam up through your body and then have it exit through of the top of your head. The destination is straight up to the Universe. Feel the energy of the laser beam connecting you to the Universal energies. These energies are being magnetized to bring you the people, places and things you need in order to realize your dreams. You have now activated the field of possibilities. I literally can feel the sensation of the beam pulling the energies down into my body. As I feel the beam, I think, "Thank you." I feel the gratitude pulsing through every cell.

What this does is magnetize the vibrations with direct access to the Universe. Imagine this beam of light connecting you with the limitless energies needed to attract the life of your dreams. If you find your mind wandering, then just bring it back to your breath and the laser beam of light. Focus on your breath and feel the beam of light pulsating throughout your body. When your focus fades, bring it back to your breath and the laser beam of light. Do this as many times as you need. Always bring your attention back to your breath and the laser beam of light. Breathe in all the possibilities, opportunities and abundance that is your life. Exhale all the negativity, obstacles and anything else that is not for your highest good and the highest good of all. It is this heart connection that raises your vibration and opens the channel to connect to your higher self and to the Universe. Be grateful and thank the Universe.

Some days are hectic, which means finding the time and space to connect to the Universe can be challenging. On those days, when time and space are in short supply, I get creative and connect when I'm in my car. I'm not meditating, as I still need my awareness on the road. What I am doing is talking to the Universe. I go through my ten gratitude's and my affirmations. I do a lot of this type of connecting in my car with the radio off. It helps with the commute and is a much more effective use of my time.

An Attitude of Gratitude

Gratitude is a high vibe feeling. If you have not practiced gratitude, I highly suggest you do. It's a game changer and is a manifester booster. It is about having appreciation for what is in your life. This is extremely important because if you cannot appreciate what you have NOW, regardless of your circumstances and you linger way too long in the feelings of "why me, why not me and this sucks," then you will not be able to manifest the life you desire. Why? You're too busy being negative about the life you have.

Gratitude is essential and should be thought of often throughout the day. There are a few things you can do to strengthen your attitude of gratitude. Before bed, I write in my manifestation journal three things that happened during the day that were amazing and one thing I could have done differently. I love this practice because it keeps me present to what is. There are times when this is hard, as some days are definitely better than others.

Gratitude can be as simple as being grateful for your morning coffee. Other days, it can be as big as being in awe of how everything is working out perfectly in your life. It's good to do this every night, but if you miss a night or two, no worries. Just get back on track. You can also create a gratitude group with three or four friends. It's fun and a great way to keep you on track. You can text each other your gratitude list at the end of the day. The reason to bring three or four people into the circle is that at least one person will remember and ignite the chain.

Next time you are waiting in line for a coffee try this quick and powerful exercise. Instead of posting on social media or checking your DM or emails, go over your gratitude list and affirmations. You can do this silently as you connect to your heart and simultaneously expand the feelings of appreciation to every cell in your body. For a long time, my affirmation was as simple as: "I AM a warm, kind and loving woman."

I had to say this until I believed. I'm happy to say I believe it with every ounce that is me.

May you manifest the life of your dreams!

Faith Enhancer	Faith Blockers
Gratitude for all that shows up in your life	Limiting thoughts and beliefs
Meditating, walks in nature	Not trusting in your journey
Believing that no matter what everything will work out	Chronic doubt

NOTES

AFTERWORD

Manifesting the Life of Your Dreams

Yay! You now hold the keys to manifesting the life you have always dreamt was possible. These keys are available to everyone; they have no prejudices. They are our gift from the Universe. This wonderful blessing is the ability to connect to the universal energies to co-create your life and your experiences.

This is The Five "F" words in action.

Play with this practice every day. Remember you can go big or small and there is no right or wrong here. Whatever is comfortable for you is right. The key is to let go of the outcome and allow the universal energies to align with your desires. Time is an earthly concept and all things happen in their own time, so be patient and have faith your dreams will manifest exactly when, how and where they are supposed to appear. Sometimes, you will experience setbacks and hurdles. I never said it was easy, but it is simple.

Whenever you find yourself struggling, slow down, meditate, take a hike, listen to your favorite music, feed yourself love and support and know the Universe is always conspiring for your highest good.

Stay present to your blockers and enhancers while scanning the lobsters in your life for possible interference. When in doubt, activate Faith and practice gratitude. Don't stress about anything as you now have a blueprint to help you get clear -- The Five "F" Words.

- **FIGURE**
- **FOCUS**
- **FEARLESS ACTION**
- **FEEL IT**
- **FAITH**

You've always had the power and now you have the keys to create the life of your dreams, GO FOR IT and DREAM BIG. The world awaits your brilliance!

LIFE HACKS

To Keep You On Track

FIGURE Out What You Want

- Go deeper than your surface desire to discover what you truly want.

- If you don't know what you want, then write a list of what you don't want.

- Live in the question until you get the answer.

- If it's not scaring you then it's not big enough.

- Don't play small, this is your life and you are worth every dream you can imagine.

- Start a manifestation journal and write in everyday

FOCUS on What You Want

- What you Focus on will ultimately manifest so choose your Focus wisely.

- Understand your why. What is your motivation for wanting what you want?

- Readjust your Focus if you find yourself discouraged or in a negative head space.

- Remember, circumstances are often out of our control. You do, however, have the power to decide how you are going to respond, think and ultimately act on those circumstances. Empower yourself to go beyond any limitations and stay focused on your destination.

- Write in your manifestation journal what you need to focus on.

Take FEARLESS Action

- Don't let fear stop you from realizing your greatness.

- Fearless doesn't mean you are not afraid; it means you do it anyway.

- Overcome fear by walking through it or diving headfirst into it.

- Take risks while listening to your intuition.

- Prepare yourself for the synchronicities that will show up in your life in the form of opportunities.

- Look for those synchronicities in every corner of your life.

- Create an action plan and/or vision board to accelerate the manifestation process.

- Educate yourself with every skill you need to set yourself up to succeed.

- Remove the lobster from your life. If you can't remove a lobster, then be very careful what you share. Keep it pleasant, superficial and all about them.

- Write in your manifestation journal.

FEEL IT As If It Already Exists

- Eliminate and or/curb all substances that dull your senses.

- Create your powerful I AM affirmation – Create several for each area of your life. Repeat them several times a day. Write them on post it notes and post on your mirror. Set a reminder on your phone every few hours. Say it until you believe it.

- Turn on the "light switch" to activate the Feeling that whatever you desire already exists.

- Let go of the outcome and allow the Universe to co-create with you. Rarely does anything manifest exactly the way we think it will. Be open to seeing life from a new perspective.

- Visualize what you want to manifest every day. As if you are watching a movie and it is happening, not in the future but in the NOW.

- Write in your manifestation journal.

FAITH is a Knowing and Believing

- Faith is very personal, and with that said, you must believe with a knowingness that what you desire is for you to have. Faith is connecting to something bigger than yourself. It is deep inside of you, and it is the Universal life force that connects all of us.

- Faith is a believing even when outside circumstances say otherwise.

- Slow down and connect with yourself and with the Universe everyday either by mediation, hikes, and/or prayer. Anything that puts you in the zone and allows you to connect to the knowing and belief that you are not alone.

- Feel gratitude every day. Pull in the "beam of light" that magnetizes the energies of co-creation.

- Limit social media and instead use this time to connect and co-create with the Universe.

Whenever you find yourself grabbing your phone to see what other people are up to, stop yourself and use this time to connect to the unseen energies that are at your disposal to co-create the life of your dreams.

- Write in your manifestation journal every evening three amazing things that happened during the day and one thing you could have done differently.

ACKNOWLEDGEMENTS

No one succeeds alone and that includes me. There are so many people who have influenced my life in so many ways that my acknowledgments could be a whole book. This list is but a small reflection of the amazing souls who have inspired me, loved me and challenged me along this incredible adventure called life. I want to thank everyone who has supported my dreams and helped my visions come alive!

My husband, Danny and my son, Eli. You two are my everything.

My speaking and writing coach Suzanne Mulroy, my editor Cindy Pearlman, my book designers Emily Tippetts, Tianne Samson and Linda Caldwell of E.M. Tippetts Book Design, my website and logo designer Anne Marie Singer. All of you amazing, beautiful woman made this all happen in such a short amount of time. I can't thank you enough.

My hair teams. You all are amazing and give one hundred and twenty five percent all the time. Meagan Herrera-Schaaf, thank you for your attention to detail and amazing talent. You are an inspiration for all of us and the strongest woman I know.

Dean Banowetz, The Hollywood Hair Guy, I can't thank you enough for your friendship and support.

Thank you, Winn Claybaugh, Dean and Co-Founder of Paul Mitchell Schools for your passion and commitment to elevating the standards of our industry and for giving me the opportunity to share my vision with the next generation of beauty professionals.

Katie Dooling and Natalie Retana, my publicists from Impact 24 PR.

Gina Greblo, Easy Updo Extensions, thank you for believing in my dream big ideas and giving me my first opportunity at spreading my vision to students at The Student Underground Hair Show. There I was able to meet Jim Cox, Paul Barry and so many others that believed in me and my vision to empower and influence cosmetology students and hairstylist to believe in themselves and manifest the life of their dreams.

I want to thank The Sharks and my mentors Robert Herjavec, Daymond John, Mark Cuban, Kevin O'Leary, Barbara Corcoran and Lori Grenier. Spending the last ten seasons on Shark Tank with all of you has been an incredible experience I could not have gotten anywhere else. You all are rock stars!

I want to thank my mentors that don't know I exist -- Rachel Hollis, Tony Robbins, Michael Bernard Beckwith, Deepak Chopra, Marianne Williamson and, of course, Oprah.

Thank You to Greg Behrendt, you, your book & your talk show changed my life forever. You told me I was worth being called a girlfriend AND a wife. To all the single ladies, please read, *He's Just Not That Into You.* It will save you a whole lot of heartache.

Thank you to my Sober Sisters. You know who you are. My world would not be the same without you in it. You are my tribe!

I want to thank my mother-in-law and late father-in-law for taking me in like your own daughter and supporting us with love.

Thank you to my husband's daughter, Ashley, our son-in-law Rex and our two beautiful grandkids. You all are the cherry on top of my sundae.

To my parents, Bob and Karen, thank you for believing in me and giving me the opportunity to shine my light in this world. I love you.

Lastly, thank you to my brother Brent, my sister-in-law Ali and all my nieces and nephew -- Shea, Kinsley, Avery and Leo. You all make my heart sing a little brighter.

ABOUT THE AUTHOR

Jerilynn Stephens has been consciously manifesting the life of her dreams for the last sixteen years. It was through study, practice and patience that she decoded the keys to manifestation. During a particularly rough time of struggling with alcohol, she hit rock bottom and picked up a book that introduced her to the world of co-creating with the Universe. Since then, love, career, joy, and money have all manifested beyond her wildest imagination. She is now on a mission to share this knowledge. She currently lives in Los Angeles with her husband, son, and their two potbelly pigs, Ricky and Lucy. When not with her family or leading a team of award-winning hairstylists as the Head Hairstylist for The Voice, Shark Tank and other top-rated shows, Jerilynn is speaking and writing about how to manifest the life of your dreams.

IN LOVING MEMORY

Two weeks before this book published, our dear sweet Ricky received his wings and made his transition to heaven. He kept us on our toes, gave us belly laughs and showered us with unconditional love. Loving Ricky is one of my family's greatest joys. We will miss him terribly and are forever grateful for his large presence in our lives.

Ricky Stephens - A Gentle Giant
November 30, 2012- October 19, 2019
RIP our sweet boy, see you in heaven

You can follow Jerilynn's life and career at

www.jerilynnstephens.com

IG @jerilynnstephens

FB Hollywood Hairstylist.

NOTES

NOTES

NOTES

NOTES

NOTES

NOTES

NOTES

NOTES

Made in the USA
San Bernardino, CA
05 March 2020

65125353R00066